ASTRONOMY
FOR THE UNDER TENS

ASTRONOMY
FOR THE UNDER TENS

Patrick Moore

GEORGE
PHILIP

British Library Cataloguing in Publication Data

Moore, Patrick, *1923 –*
    Astronomy for the under tens.
    1. Astronomy – For children
    I. Title
    520
ISBN 0-540-01181-9

Copyright © Patrick Moore 1986
Reprinted 1987
Second edition © Patrick Moore 1989

This book was designed and produced by
The Oregon Press Limited, Faraday House,
8-10 Charing Cross Road, London WC2H 0HG
for George Philip Limited, 59 Grosvenor Street,
London W1X 9DA

Design: Mick Keates
Illustrations: Paul Doherty
Production: Hugh Allan

Filmset by Ampersand Typesetting Limited,
56 Old Christchurch Road, Bournemouth, Dorset BH1 1LL
Printed and bound by Purnell Book Production Limited,
Paulton, Bristol BS18 5LQ

Author's acknowledgments

As on many previous occasions, I am most grateful to Paul Doherty for his splendid illustrations. I am also deeply indebted to Mary Anne Sanders for her invaluable help throughout.

My grateful thanks are due to James Turner who, at the age of seven, read through the manuscript of this book and made many helpful suggestions, all of which I have followed.

CONTENTS

CHAPTER 1
LOOKING AT THE SKY

What is a star? Why is the Sun so hot? Why does the Moon seem to change its shape? And why is the sky blue? These are some of the questions I hope to answer in this book.

Men and women who study the sky, and everything in it, are called astronomers. Astronomy began a very long time ago, when there were no towns or even farms. But at first nobody knew what the Earth was really like, and they thought that it must be flat, with the sky moving round it once a day.

This is not true, as everyone now knows. The Earth is shaped like a ball. It is 12,756 kilometres (7926 miles) across, so that if you go from England to Australia, almost halfway round the surface of the world, you will travel about 20,000 kilometres (12,400 miles).

The Sun is also shaped like a ball – but it is much bigger than the Earth. The picture shows how large the Sun is compared with the Earth. You could take a million balls the size of the Earth and pack them inside the Sun, leaving plenty of room to spare.

The Sun is hot. It sends us all our light and heat, and without it we would not be here. The bright face of the Sun is at a temperature of nearly 6000°C – twice as hot as the hottest coal fire, and the temperature increases towards its centre to at least 14 million degrees C (perhaps rather more).

The Moon is quite different. It is a quarter of the diameter of the Earth, and is much closer to us than the Sun. If you fly ten times round the world, you will travel a distance which is as far as going from the Earth to the Moon. The Moon has no light of its own, and shines only because it is lit up by the Sun. If the Sun stopped shining, the Moon would disappear too. Luckily, this cannot happen.

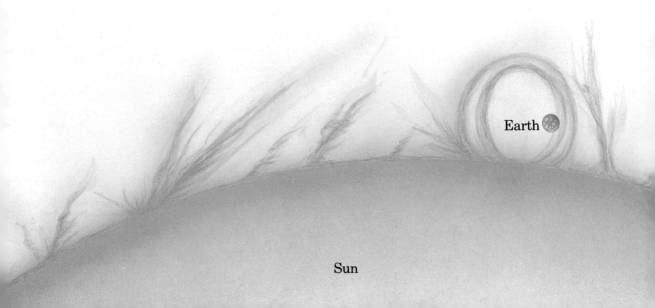

Earth

Sun

The Earth is a *planet,* moving round the Sun. Eight other planets are known, of which the brightest are Venus, Mars, Jupiter and Saturn. Planets look like stars but, as with the Moon, they shine only because they are lit up by the Sun – just as a tennis ball will shine if you light it up with a torch in a dark room.

The Earth takes one year to go right round the Sun. The other planets take different times, so that their 'years' are not the same as ours.

The distance between the Earth and the Sun is 150 million kilometres (93 million miles). This is a very long way indeed. If you could drive from the Earth to the Sun, keeping up a speed of 100 kilometres (just over 60 miles) an hour and never stopping, the journey would take you over 170 years.

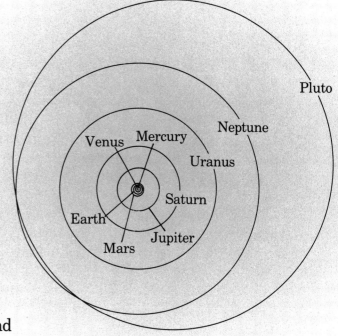

Plan of the Solar System

Yet the Sun is only a star, and all the stars you can see on any dark night are suns. Like our Sun, they are very hot and powerful. They look so much fainter than the Sun only because they are much further away from us. They do not move round our Sun as our planets do, and in fact many stars may have planets of their own.

It is only at night time that you can see the stars and the planets. This is because during the daytime the sky is too bright, so that the stars do not show up. The Earth is surrounded by air, and this air spreads the Sun's light around, making the sky look blue. If you point a telescope in the right direction, you can see stars in the daytime – but it is very dangerous to look straight at the Sun with or without a telescope, because the intense light and heat would damage your eyes and can cause blindness.

The air does not stretch upwards very far. If you could climb Mount Everest, which is about 8 kilometres (5 miles) high, you would find that the air would be too thin for you to breathe. Above a few hundred kilometres there is no air at all. Men and women have now travelled in space (where there is no air), and twelve men have even been to the Moon, but they have to use rockets, not aircraft.

The sky seems to move round, so that the Sun rises in the east and sets in the west. This is because the Earth is spinning; so let us now see just how our world moves.

CHAPTER 2
HOW THE EARTH MOVES

The Earth travels round the Sun in a path which is very nearly a circle. The astronomer's name for such a path is *orbit*, so that in a year the Earth moves all the way round its orbit. It also spins round, making one turn in just under 24 hours. When we are on the side of the Earth facing the Sun, it is daylight; when we are on the other side of the Earth, we have our night.

Because the Earth's orbit is not quite a circle, we are a little closer to the Sun in December, around Christmastime, than we are in June. This may seem strange, because in December it is winter in Britain and the days and nights are much colder than in summer, but the Earth's *seasons* are caused in quite another way.

The Earth spins on what we call its *axis*. You can make a model of this by taking a ball of wool, or something just as soft, and sticking a pencil through it. If you spin the pencil, the ball will turn round, so that the pencil has become the axis of the ball. This is shown in the picture, with the Earth taking the place of the ball of wool. The north pole is marked by N, and the south pole by S. The equator divides the Earth into two halves or hemispheres; the British Isles lie in the northern half, Australia in the southern.

The Earth's axis is tipped over to one side relative to the line of its orbit. In the next drawing, look first at the left-hand picture. The Earth's north pole is tipped towards the Sun, and the south pole is tipped away from the Sun, so that the northern part of the Earth is getting more of the Sun's heat. In the right-hand picture the north pole is tipped away from the Sun, and the northern hemisphere has its winter. The Earth is over 3 million kilometres (nearly 2 million miles) closer to the Sun in December than in June, but this is not enough to make much difference to the seasons.

If you travel to the north pole, you will have a 'day' lasting for six months, between March and September, while for the other six months of the year it will be dark. The picture shows why this is so. All through our summer, the light from the Sun can reach the north pole all the time, and no sunlight at all can reach the south pole, because the solid body of the Earth gets in the way. From September to March things are the other way round, with the north pole in darkness and the south pole in sunlight.

Because the Earth spins on its axis

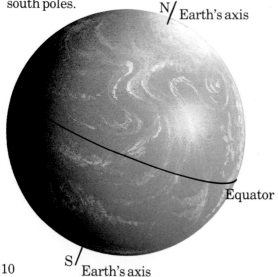

The Earth is spinning round like a top, making one full turn in 24 hours. The world is divided into two halves by the equator. The *axis*, round which the Earth spins, is marked by the north and south poles.

N / Earth's axis

Equator

S / Earth's axis

from west to east, the sky seems to move round from east to west, taking the Sun, the Moon and everything else with it. Daylight lasts longer than night time in summer because the Sun is higher in the sky, and takes more time to cross from one horizon to the other.

If the Earth were further away from the Sun, the year

THE SEASONS. In northern summer (left) the north pole of the Earth is tipped toward the Sun; in southern summer (right) it is the turn of the south pole. This is the cause of the seasons. In between winter and summer, the days and nights are equal all over the world.

would be longer. The planet Mars has a bigger orbit than ours, so that it takes 687 days to make one journey round the Sun. The furthest away of the big planets, Neptune, is so distant that it takes almost 165 years to make one full journey.

The Earth moves round the Sun not in exactly 365 days, but in 365.26. This means that our calendar of 365 days is not quite right, and we have to add an extra day every 4 years to make the correction. This is why in 'Leap Years' February has 29 days instead of 28. To find out if a year is a Leap Year, divide by 4; if there is no remainder, then we have a Leap Year. (A 'century' year such as 1900 or 2000 has to be divided by 400. Thus 1900 was not a Leap Year, but 2000 will be.)

THE SUN'S PATH. As seen from Britain and other countries in the northern part of the world, the Sun rises higher in summer than in winter. In the picture, we see the apparent path of the Sun, as seen from Britain in December. In summer the Sun reaches a much higher point when due south. Conditions in southern countries, such as Australia, are exactly opposite.

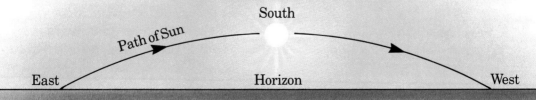

CHAPTER 3
HOW ASTRONOMERS WORK

When you look up at the sky, you can see the Sun, the Moon, the planets and some of the stars. If you want to see them more clearly you must use a *telescope*, or a pair of *binoculars*.

Telescopes used by astronomers are of two kinds. The first kind of telescope, the *refractor*, collects the light by using a piece of glass which we call a *lens* or *object-glass*. Let us begin by looking at the Moon. In the picture, the light coming from the Moon hits the lens and passes through it. The lens bunches the rays of light up, and brings them together. At this point, marked F in the picture, an image of the Moon is formed. The next thing to do is to make the image larger, and this means using a smaller lens which works in just the same way as a magnifying glass. When you look into this smaller lens, which we call the *eyepiece*, we see an enlarged view of the Moon. Of course the same is true if

How a refractor works

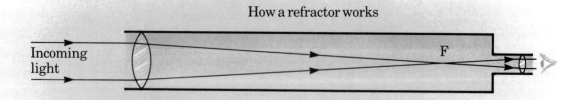

Incoming light

F

you look at anything else in the sky, though the stars are so far away that no telescope will show them as more than specks of light.

A pair of binoculars is nothing more than two small telescopes of this kind joined together. With binoculars, you can use both your eyes instead of only one.

The other kind of telescope, the *reflector*, works in a different way. The light comes straight down on to a mirror, which is curved. This mirror sends the light back on to a smaller mirror, which is flat. This flat smaller mirror sends the rays of light into the side of the telescope, where the image is formed, and can then be made larger by an eyepiece. With a telescope of this sort, you have to look 'into' it instead of 'up' it.

An astronomer's telescope turns everything upside down. With a telescope used for looking at birds, or ships out to sea, an extra lens is put in to turn the image the right way up again, and this is always done with binoculars (it would be very strange to see people walking about on their heads!). But for astronomy, we want to collect as

How a reflector works

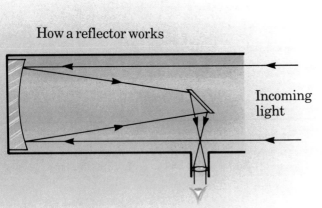

Incoming light

much light as we can, and every time light goes through a lens it becomes a little fainter, so that with a telescope used for looking at the sky the extra lens is left out. After all, it does not matter whether the Moon looks upside down or the right way up.

The biggest telescope in the world has a mirror 6 metres (236-inch) across. It has been made by the Russians, but it does not work very well, and the biggest really good telescope is in America; it has a 5-metre (200-inch) mirror.

Large telescopes are kept inside *observatories*. When the telescope is to be used, part of the roof of the observatory is opened, so that the telescope can see the sky. Most of the world's great observatories have been built on or near the tops of mountains, where the air is thin and does not blot out the light coming from the stars. For example, there are several big telescopes on the top of a volcano on the island of Hawaii, in the Pacific, at a height of 4205 metres 14,000 feet above sea level. If you go there, you must remember not to run about, because the air is so thin that you will quickly become out of breath.

It is not often that an astronomer in a big observatory looks through a telescope. Instead, he uses the telescope to take photographs. In this way he can learn much more than he could just by looking through the eyepiece.

200-inch Palomar reflector

If you want to buy a telescope for astronomy, it will mean spending a good deal of money. Many people do not want to do this, and the best thing to do is to buy a pair of binoculars, which are much more useful than a very small telescope, and will show you the stars very well.

Remember that if you do buy a telescope, it need not be in an observatory – but no telescope should ever be left outdoors unless it is covered up to stop it getting damp.

200-inch Observatory dome

CHAPTER 4
THE SUN

The Sun is not solid. It is made up of gas, and it is so hot that you should never look at it with any telescope or binoculars. You should not even look straight at the Sun without a telescope, unless you hold up a piece of very dark glass in front of your eyes.

The only safe way to observe the Sun is to turn a telescope towards it, without looking through the eyepiece, and then send the Sun's image on to a piece of white card held behind the telescope. The picture shows you how to do it – but never try it unless you have somebody with you to make sure that you are not doing anything wrong.

Patrick Moore observing the Sun.

Like the Earth, the Sun spins round on its axis, but it does so much more slowly, and takes about four weeks to make one full turn. We can prove this by looking at sunspots, which are dark patches on the bright face of the Sun. Some of them may become much larger than the Earth, and they often appear in groups. No sunspot can last for more than a few months at most, and there are times when there are no spots at all. A sunspot is cooler than the surrounding surface; it is due to magnetic effects.

As the Sun spins, the spots are carried across the bright face, though not quickly enough for you to notice their movements except from one day to the next. Look at these two pictures, which show sunspots that I saw using my telescope to throw the Sun's image on to a piece of card in the way that I have

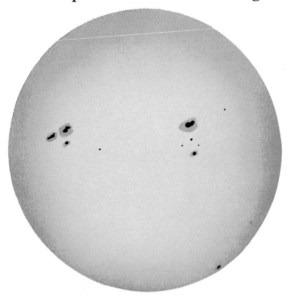

First observation

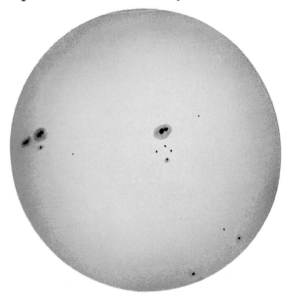

Second observation

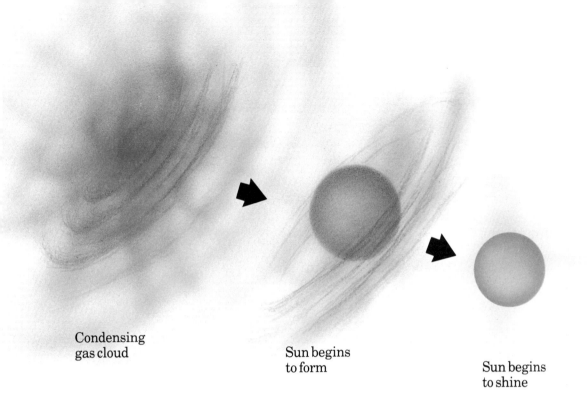

Condensing
gas cloud

Sun begins
to form

Sun begins
to shine

HOW THE SUN WAS BORN. The Sun was born inside what is called a 'nebula', which is a word meaning 'cloud'. The cloud began to shrink, because of the force of gravity, and the inside became so hot that at last the Sun started to shine.

shown you. In the left-hand illustration you can see a group of spots. The right-hand illustration was made two days later, and the spots have moved. It takes a spot about two weeks to cross from one side of the Sun's face to the other; it will then go round on to the far side, where we cannot see it, but in another two weeks it will come back, if it still exists.

How does the Sun shine? It is not burning in the same way as a coal fire. If it did, it would not last for very long before burning away, but we know that the Sun is very old, so that we must think of something else.

Astronomers are now sure that they know the answer. Inside the Sun, one kind of gas is being changed into another. Every time this happens, the Sun sends out a little light and heat, and it loses a little 'weight'. This is what keeps the Sun shining. It loses 4 million tons in weight every second.

Can you imagine how much 4 million trucks would weigh, if each truck carried a ton of coal? Yet this is the amount of weight which the Sun is losing every second. Luckily the Sun is so big that it will go on shining much as it does now for thousands of millions of years in the future.

We believe that the Sun began its life inside a 'cloud' of dust and gas. At first it was not enough to shine, but as it became smaller it also became hotter, and turned into the Sun we know today.

CHAPTER 5
ECLIPSES

Now let us see how the Sun and the Moon can appear to move behind and in front of each other.

The Earth moves round the Sun, while the Moon moves round the Earth. The Moon has no light of its own, so that when its dark side is turned towards us we cannot see it. Because the Moon is so much closer than the Sun, it looks the same size in the sky, just as a tennis ball will look as big as a soccer ball if the soccer ball is further away from you. This means that we can sometimes see what we call an *eclipse* of the Sun.

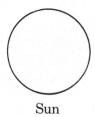

Sun

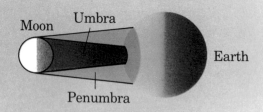

How a total solar eclipse occurs

The picture shows the Earth, the Moon and the Sun in a straight line, with the Moon in the middle. (I have not been able to draw the picture to the right scale, because the Sun is too big, but this does not matter.) At such times the Moon gets in the way of the Sun, and its shadow touches the Earth, so that if you are inside the shadow the Sun is covered up by the Moon, causing an eclipse.

A total eclipse, when the Sun lies directly behind the Moon, is a wonderful sight. The dark face of the Moon is surrounded by the Sun's *corona,* which looks like a white mist often stretching across the sky, and we can also see red patches which were once called Red Flames but are now known as *prominences.* They are clouds of very hot gas above the Sun's surface. During a total eclipse, the sky becomes so dark that the stars come out – the only time you can see stars in the daytime without using a telescope.

The Moon takes less than four weeks to go round the Earth, so why do we not see an eclipse every month? The reason is that the orbit of the Moon is tipped – not by much, but by enough to stop the Earth, the Moon and the Sun moving into a straight

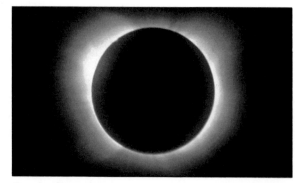

Total solar eclipse

16

line very often. The last total eclipse to be seen from the British Isles was that of 1927, and there will not be another until 11 August 1999, though total eclipses do occur over other parts of the world. I took the photograph shown here in 1983, when there was a total eclipse of the Sun seen from the island of Java in Indonesia.

No total eclipse can last for more than a few minutes. They are very important, and astronomers are always ready to go on long journeys to see them. It is bad luck if the sky is cloudy at the wrong moment, as often happens!

If the Moon does not hide the Sun completely, we have a partial eclipse, while at other times there may be a ring of sunlight left showing around the dark face of the Moon. Eclipses of this kind are not nearly so interesting, because it is not possible to see the corona or the prominences.

Thousands of years ago, people were frightened of eclipses. They did not know why they happened. In China it was even thought that a hungry dragon was trying to eat the Sun. Today we are not at all frightened by eclipses, but they are always worth seeing, and it is a pity that they do not happen every month.

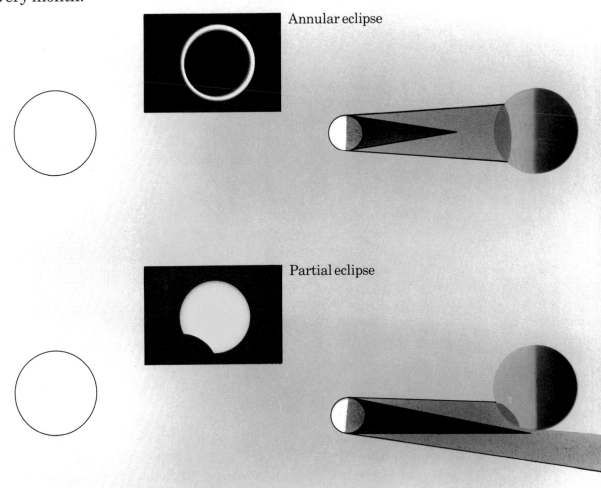

Annular eclipse

Partial eclipse

CHAPTER 6
ROCKETS INTO SPACE

The Moon is much closer to us than anything else in the sky, but it is still a long way away. If you use a tennis ball to take the place of the Earth, wrap a string round it ten times, and then unwrap the string and put a table tennis ball on the far end, you will have made yourself a good model of the Earth and the Moon to the same scale.

If we want to fly to the Moon we cannot use an aircraft – because an aircraft will not work unless there is air round it, and there is no air above a height of a few kilometres. The only way to go into space is to use rockets.

Think about a firework rocket, of the kind we use on Guy Fawkes night or other celebrations. A rocket of this sort is made up of a cardboard tube filled with gunpowder. When you light the powder, it starts to burn, and sends out hot gas through the end of the rocket. As the gas streams out, it 'kicks' the tube away from it, and the rocket flies.

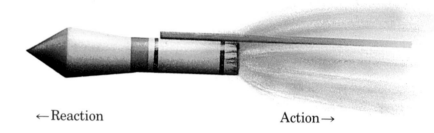

←Reaction   Action→

To show what I mean, stand on a book and jump off it. As you jump one way, the book will move in the opposite direction, because of the kick you gave it. This would still happen even if there were no air round you. Just as you kicked the book, so the gas kicks the rocket – and this means that rockets will work very well in empty space.

Of course, a Moon rocket is very different from a firework, and it has a very special kind of engine. The first space rockets were sent up many years ago, and what we may call the real Space Age began in October 1957, when the Russians launched a man-made moon or *artificial satellite*. It was only about the size of a soccer ball, but it carried a radio set, and it went round and round the Earth above the top of the air.

Sputnik 1 launched by the Russians on 4 October 1957.

If you tie a cotton reel on to the end of a string and whirl it round, the cotton reel will not fall, but will keep on moving round your hand. There is no string holding an artificial satellite to the Earth, but so long as it goes on moving it will not fall – and it keeps moving because there is nothing to stop it. Since 1957 many of these artificial satellites have been sent up, and you can often see them crossing the sky like slowly moving stars.

In 1961 the first space man went up in a rocket and travelled round the Earth. He was a Russian, named Yuri Gagarin. Since then there have been many other space flights, and men have stayed up for almost a year at a time.

Saturn V, a very powerful rocket used to launch many spaceships – including the Apollo missions to the Moon.

Life in a spaceship is very strange. You seem to have no weight; if you hold out a book and then let go, the book will not fall, but will simply stay in front of you. There is no up and no down. You cannot pour out a glass of water, because the water has no weight. It takes some time to get used to eating and drinking!

Going to the Moon in a rocket means a journey lasting several days. The first landing on the Moon was made in 1969 by the Americans Neil Armstrong and Edwin Aldrin, in their spaceship Apollo 11. There have been six Moon trips altogether, and for the last three the spacemen took Moon cars with them so that they could drive around. The Moon cars were left behind, so that one day they will be used again. We know just where they are, and there is nothing to damage them, because on the airless Moon there are no storms and no rain.

The planets move round the Sun, not round the Earth as the Moon does, and they are much further away. To travel to a planet takes many weeks, and for the biggest planets the journey lasts for years. So far, we have not been able to send men any further than the Moon, though unmanned rockets have been able to go to most of the planets and tell us what they are really like.

The Lunar Module was the part of the spaceship which landed on the Moon and which took the astronauts back to their main space-craft. The last three Apollo missions took with them a Moon car or Lunar Rover used by the astronauts to drive about on the Moon.

CHAPTER 7
THE MOON

You cannot always see the Moon. For part of each month it is out of view, and even when it can be seen it may not show us the whole of its face.

Because the Moon is lit up by the Sun, only half of it can shine at any one time, just as you can light up only half a soccer ball by shining a torch on it. This is why the Moon shows what we call its *phases,* from new to full.

In the picture below, we see the Sun and the Earth, with the Moon's path round the Earth. (I cannot draw it to the right scale, because the Sun is 400 times as far from us as the Moon.) The dark side of the Moon has been blacked in, and the sunlit half has been left white.

In position 1, the Moon has its dark or night side turned towards us, and the Moon is new; we cannot see it at all, unless it passes straight in front of the Sun and causes an eclipse. As the Moon moves on, we start to see part of the bright side. The Moon becomes a crescent in the evening sky, then a half (position 2) and then a three-quarter shape. At position 3 the Moon has its sunlit face turned towards us, and is full. It then becomes three-quarters once more, then half (position 4) and then a crescent before arriving back in position 1. There is one new moon and one full moon every 29½ days.

If the full moon is lined up with the Earth, as shown in the next picture, it passes into the Earth's shadow, and there is an eclipse of the Moon – which is

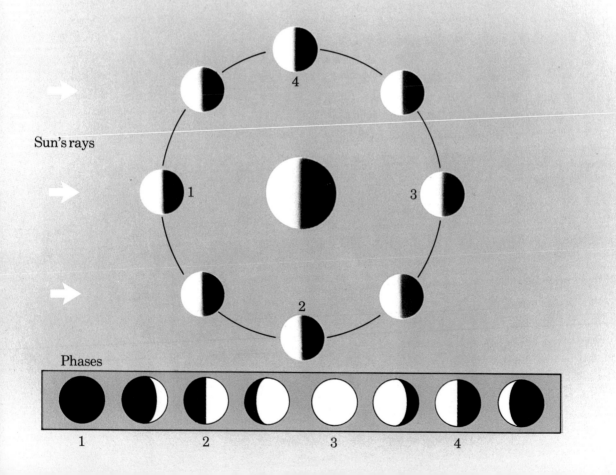

Sun's rays

Phases

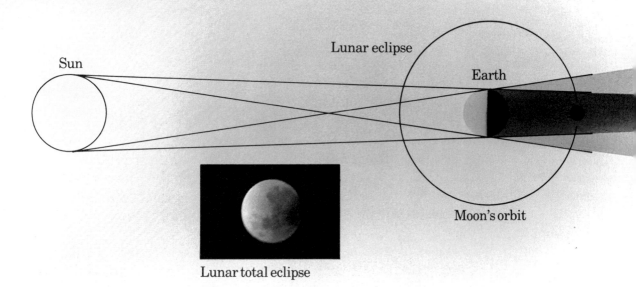

Sun

Lunar eclipse

Earth

Moon's orbit

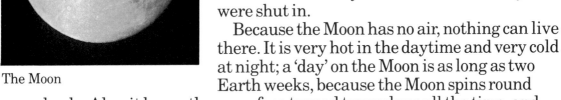

Lunar total eclipse

quite different from an eclipse of the Sun. The sunlight is cut off from the Moon, and the Moon becomes very faint until it passes out of the shadow again. Eclipses of this kind may be either total or partial; they are seen more often than eclipses of the Sun (see pages 16 and 17).

It is easy to see that there are bright and dark patches on the Moon. The dark patches are called 'seas', but there has never been any water in them, and they are really great dry plains.

Telescopes also show that the Moon is covered with *craters*. A crater is a hole with a wall round it, and sometimes a mountain in the middle. Some of them are very big: well over 150 kilometres (93 miles) across, much larger than any craters on the Earth. Yet they are not so deep as they look, and if you were standing inside one of them you would not feel that you were shut in.

Because the Moon has no air, nothing can live there. It is very hot in the daytime and very cold at night; a 'day' on the Moon is as long as two Earth weeks, because the Moon spins round

The Moon

very slowly. Also, it keeps the same face turned towards us all the time, and there is part of the Moon that we can never see.

We know why this is so. The Moon spins round in the same time that it takes to complete one journey round the Earth. If you walk round a chair, turning so as to keep your head turned towards it, anyone sitting in the chair will not be able to see the back of your neck; in the same way, we on Earth cannot see the back of the Moon. But by now the spaceships have sent back pictures of it, and we have drawn very good maps of it.

The Moon is a strange place. If you go there the sky is black, and you can see the Earth in the sky, looking like a large blue and white ball.

CHAPTER 8
THE HOT PLANETS

Now let us leave the Earth and its Moon, and look at the other planets that move round the Sun.

As soon as you look at a plan of what we call the *Solar System* you can see that the planets make up two separate groups. The first group contains Mercury, Venus, the Earth and Mars; than comes a wide gap in which move many very small worlds, and then we have the really big planets Jupiter, Saturn, Uranus and Neptune, together with one small planet, Pluto.

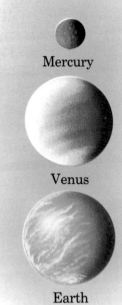

Mercury

Venus

Earth

Mercury is the closest planet to the Sun. It is never very easy to see, because it always stays in the same part of the sky as the Sun; you can sometimes find it either low in the west after sunset or low in the east before sunrise, but it is difficult to find without knowing exactly where to look.

Mercury is smaller than the Earth, and not much bigger than the Moon. It has no air, no water and no life, and because it is so near the Sun it is very hot in the daytime. If you could put a tin kettle on to the rocks, the kettle would melt. Mercury's 'year' is only 88 days long.

From the Earth we can never see Mercury well. One spaceship has flown past it and has sent back pictures showing mountains, craters and plains not unlike those of the Moon, but there is no chance of men going there, at least for a long time yet.

The next planet, Venus, is quite different. It is almost as big as the Earth, and it is always bright, because when closest to us it is only about a hundred times as far away as the Moon. It is best seen in the west after sunset, or in the east before dawn, but it is so brilliant that you can often find it even when it is not dark.

With a telescope, it can be seen that Venus behaves very much like the Moon, showing phases or changes of shape. The reasons are

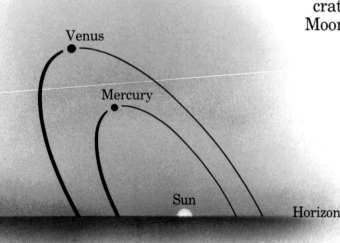

HOW THE INNER PLANETS MOVE. Mercury and Venus are closer to the Sun than we are so they always keep in the same part of the sky as the Sun. Venus, further out than Mercury, can move further away from the Sun in the sky.

much the same. In the picture I have shown the Sun, the Earth and Venus. When Venus is in position 1 its dark side faces us, and we cannot see it. In position 2 we see half the bright side. When Venus reaches position 3 it is full, but as it is then almost behind the Sun it is out of view. At position 4 Venus is a half again, and then becomes a crescent before returning to position 1. The changes take place much more slowly than those of the Moon, because Venus takes nearly 225 days to go round the sun.

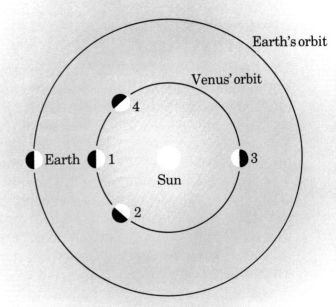

The phases of Venus.

Though the 'year' is so short, the 'day' on Venus is much longer than ours. We have found that the planet spins round from east to west, so that if you could go there and look upward the Sun would rise in the west and set in the east.

But this is not the whole story. If you went to Venus you would never see the Sun at all, because the 'air' is too thick and too cloudy. The spaceships that have been sent there have told us that the planet is very hot indeed – even hotter than Mercury – and that the air is not made up of gases that we could breathe. There are high mountains, valleys and craters, but there is no water, and the clouds are made up of very dangerous stuff called *sulphuric acid*. The sky is bright orange, and there are rocks everywhere. It is also thought that there are great volcanoes, and that thunder and lightning never cease.

In every way Venus seems to be an unfriendly place. It may look beautiful when seen in the sky, but there is no chance that we will be able to go there.

The surface of Venus in the region of an active volcano. Imaginary view.

CHAPTER 9
THE RED PLANET MARS

The third planet in the Sun's family is the Earth upon which we live. Next we come to Mars, which is smaller than the Earth but much larger than the Moon. It takes 687 days to go round the Sun, but the day on Mars is only half an hour longer than ours.

In the sky Mars looks like a red star. It cannot always be seen, as it is sometimes on the other side of the Sun, but when at its best it is very bright indeed. Because it is the colour of blood, the early stargazers named it after their god of war.

Through a telescope Mars shows red patches, dark spots and white caps at the poles. Our poles are ice-covered, and so are those of Mars. The red patches have been called deserts, but they are not like the Earth's deserts. They are cold instead of hot, because Mars is so much further from the Sun. We used to think that the dark patches were old sea beds filled with plants, but we now know that this is not true. All that has happened is that the red dust has been blown away by the winds, so that we can see the darker rocks underneath.

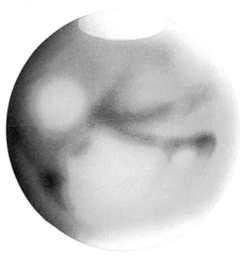

Mars as seen through a telescope.

Mars and the Earth to the same scale.

The air on Mars is very thin, and we could not breathe it. There are no seas or ponds, but at least there is plenty of ice, which is simply frozen water.

Not so very long ago it was still thought that there might be life on Mars.

Some astronomers looked at Mars through telescopes and drew straight lines crossing the red deserts, which they believed to be canals built to pump water from the ice-covered poles through to the warmer parts of the planet. We now know that there are no canals, and we have quite given up the idea of men on Mars. Dust stops the 'blue' part of sunlight and lets the 'red' part through – as we know on Earth; the setting sun looks red. Several spaceships have been there. Two of them, known as Vikings 1 and 2, have landed in the deserts and have

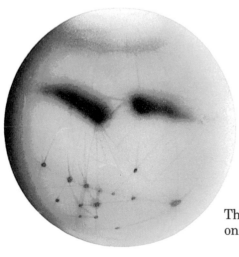

The 'canals' on Mars.

sent back pictures. The land is rocky and usually frozen. The sky is not blue like that of the Earth or orange like that of Venus; it is pink, because of the dust which floats in the air.

The Viking spaceships did their best to find out if there could be any life on Mars. They sent out scoops and collected some of the surface dust, taking it inside the spaceship and studying it. No life was found, and it is now thought that Mars is probably a dead world.

There are many craters on Mars, and there are also great volcanoes, one of which is three times as high as our Mount Everest. The winds can be quite fast, and sometimes there are dust storms which spread out across Mars.

Another way in which Mars is different from the Earth is that it has two moons instead of one. Both are very small, and hard to see except with big telescopes; the spaceships have told us that they are rocky and cratered. They will not be of much use in lighting up the dark nights on Mars.

In spite of its thin air and its coldness, Mars is much less unlike the Earth than any of the other planets, and it should be possible to send men there. Perhaps this will happen within the next thirty or forty years.

View of the surface of Mars with a pink sky and a rocky red surface taken from one of the two Viking spacecraft.

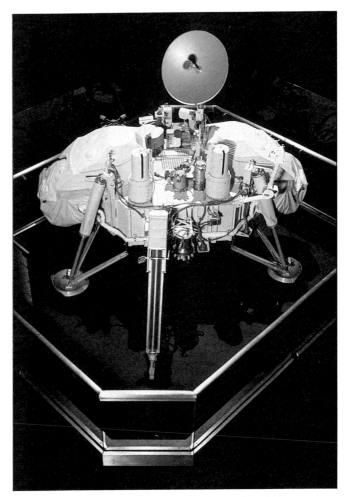

Viking Lander. Two of these craft landed on Mars in 1976. There were no men on board, but there were cameras and measuring instruments.

CHAPTER 10
THE GIANT PLANETS

Mercury
Venus
Earth
Mars
Jupiter   Asteroids
Saturn
Uranus
Neptune
Pluto
Jupiter
Moons

Beyond Mars we come to the small planets or asteroids, only one of which, Vesta, is very visible with the naked eye. Probably they are made up of material left over when the main planets were formed.

Jupiter, next in order, is much the largest and most important of all the planets: it could hold over a thousand Earths. It has a short 'day' less than 10 hours long, but its 'year' is nearly 12 times as long as ours. Through a telescope it is seen as a yellowish, flattened disk, crossed by dark lines or 'cloud belts'. There is also one famous marking, the Great Red Spot, which we now know to be a great storm, and like the rest of the surface it is very cold, though Jupiter is hot inside.

Jupiter has sixteen moons. Four of them are so bright that you can see them with any telescope, and three of them are larger than our Moon. Before the Space Age we did not know much about them, but by now four rockets have flown past Jupiter and sent back pictures. One of the bright moons, named Io, is very red, and there are powerful volcanoes there; the other three big moons are covered with ice. Jupiter is not a world which we can ever visit. There is nothing solid upon which a space-ship could land, and there are also very dangerous belts of *radiation* which would quickly kill anyone who went too close. Far outside the orbit of Jupiter we come to Saturn, which in some ways is not unlike Jupiter; it too has a surface made up of gas, and we can see belts and spots. Saturn is smaller than Jupiter, but much larger than the Earth. Its *year* is 29½ times longer than ours, but the *day* is shorter, because Saturn spins round in less than eleven hours. Saturn has a wonderful system of rings, made up of pieces of ice moving

JUPITER. The biggest planet with a diameter over ten times that of the Earth.

Earth

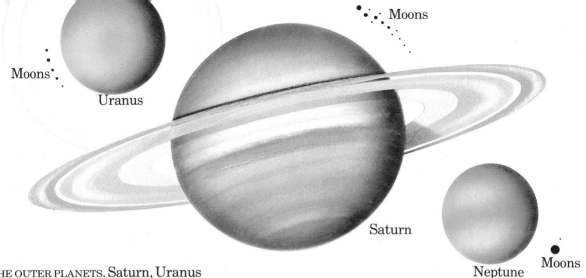

Moons

Uranus

Moons

Saturn

Neptune Moons

THE OUTER PLANETS. Saturn, Uranus and Neptune are much larger than the Earth. Here they are drawn to the same scale as Jupiter on the opposite page. Saturn's largest moon, Titan, is bigger than our Moon and also bigger than the planet Mercury.

round the planet. They can be seen with a small telescope, and there is nothing else quite like them in the Solar System. Of the twenty moons of Saturn much the most interesting is Titan, which has a dense *air,* though it is so cold that we do not believe there can be any life on it.

Three space-ships have now passed by Saturn, and one of them went to pass by the next planet, Uranus. Uranus is a very unusual place. It is 'tipped on its side', so that at the moment one pole faces the Sun, and the poles are warmer than the equator! Each pole has a 'day' lasting for 42 Earth years, and an equally long night. Uranus has a gaseous surface, with few clouds. It is faint, but just visible with the naked eye if you know where to find it. It has 15 moons, all smaller than our Moon, together with a system of ten dark rings.

The last big planet is Neptune, which cannot be seen with the naked eye; it is a little smaller than Uranus and much further away, so that it takes 165 years to go round the Sun. Finally, there is Pluto, a very small world (smaller than our Moon), which may not be a proper planet. It is very faint.

There may well be several more planets beyond Pluto and Neptune, but even if they exist they will be very difficult to find.

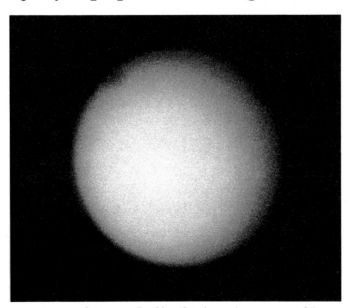

URANUS, as photographed by the American space ship Voyager 2 in January 1986. Uranus is faint and there are few markings on it.

27

CHAPTER 11
COMETS AND SHOOTING STARS

Have you ever seen a brilliant comet, with a shining head and a tail stretching right across the sky? Almost certainly not, because there have been very few of them for the last fifty years. But comets are members of the Solar System, and they may at any time take us by surprise.

A comet is not solid, like a planet. The centre of it is thought to be made up of ice, together with pieces of rock and dust. When the comet comes in towards the Sun, the ice starts to melt, and the comet develops a head made up of tiny particles and thin gas, which surrounds the ice and hides it. There also may be a tail, and indeed one comet seen many years ago had no fewer than six tails.

Comets go round the Sun, but their paths are not almost circular, as the orbits of the planets are.

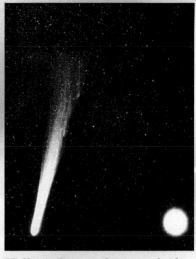

Halley's Comet photographed on its last visit in 1910. The bright object, bottom right, is the planet Venus.

A comet's path is very long and narrow, as you can see from this picture, which shows the orbit of the most famous comet of all – known as Halley's Comet, because it was the great English astronomer Edmond Halley, who lived from 1656 to 1742, who first found out how it moves. Halley's Comet takes 76 years to go round the Sun, but we can see it for only a few years at a time, because a comet shines by reflected sunlight, and when it is a long way away it is too faint to be seen at all. Halley's Comet was on view in

Tail of gas and dust

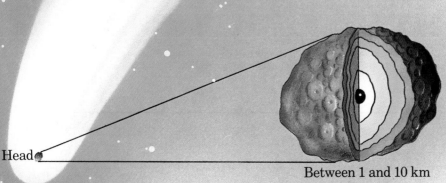

Head

Between 1 and 10 km average

Inside the nucleus of a comet

1910, and again in 1985-6. Not all comets have tails, and many of them look like nothing more than small, shining patches in the sky.

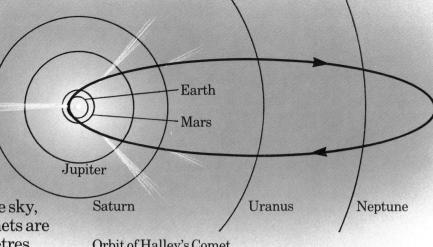

Orbit of Halley's Comet.
Note tail always points away from Sun.

If you see something moving quickly across the sky, it cannot be a comet. Comets are always millions of kilometres away, and have to be watched for many hours before they can be seen to have moved against the background of stars.

As a comet moves along, it scatters 'dust' behind it. These tiny pieces of 'dust' are called meteors. Most of them are much smaller than pin heads, and we cannot see them unless they dash into the top part of the Earth's air. The meteor quickly burns away, and leaves a streak of light which we call a shooting star. Meteors are most common each August.

Now and then the Earth meets a larger body, which lands without being burned away, and is then called a meteorite.

The biggest meteorite known to us weighs over 60 tons, and is still lying where it fell centuries

Brilliant fireball seen in 1980 over Wales and North-west England.

A shower of shooting stars.

ago in Africa. In Arizona, in the United States, there is a large crater which was made by a meteorite, luckily before there were any men there. If a meteorite hit a city such as London it would cause a great deal of damage and kill many people, but it is very unlikely that this will happen. We do not know of any case of a man or woman being badly hurt by a tumbling meteorite.

CHAPTER 12
THE STARS

Twinkle, twinkle, little star,
How I wonder what you are!

Most people have heard this old rhyme. Today we know that the stars are suns, and that they are so far away that they look only like dots of light. They make patterns or *constellations,* and these constellations do not change, so that they look the same now as they must have done in the time of Jesus Christ.

To explain why this is so, think about a bird flying about among the trees and also a jet aircraft very high above you. The jet is moving much faster than the bird, but it seems to travel much more slowly simply because it is at a greater distance. The rule is 'the further, the slower', and the stars are so far away that compared with each other they do not seem to move at all. (This is not quite

The Milky Way

true, but the changes in the constellations are so slight that you will certainly not be able to notice them.) Among the most famous of the constellations are the Great Bear, the Bull and the Dragon.

We must remember that the stars in any constellation are not really close together, because the stars are at very different distances from us. Imagine that you are looking at two soccer balls, one close to you and the other much further away; to you they will look as if they are side by side. It is the same with the stars, and we could easily make up different constellation figures if we wanted to do so.

The Great Bear has seven fairly bright stars arranged in a pattern which some people call the Plough or the Big Dipper. Two of its stars point upward to another star of about the same brightness, which we call Polaris or the Pole Star because it is very close to the north pole of the sky as seen from the Earth. Early in this book I talked about the Earth's axis, around which the world spins. The pole of the sky lies in line with this axis, so that everything seems to move round it once in 24 hours, and the Pole Star itself seems to stand almost still. Of course the stars do not really move round the pole; it is simply the result of the Earth's rotation.

The Plough is not far from the pole, and it never sets over the British Isles, so that you can always see it whenever the sky is clear and dark, but from southern hemisphere countries such as Australia it can never be seen at all, because it does not rise above the horizon. In the same way, we in Britain

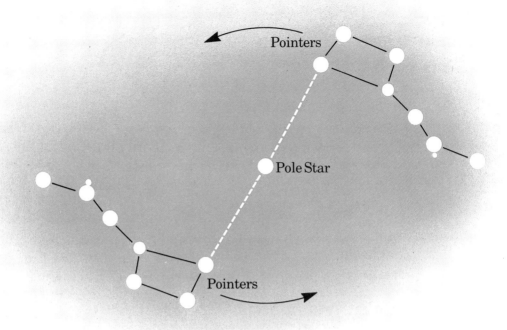

How the Plough seems to move

can never see some of the constellations of the far south, such as the famous Southern Cross.

Another well-known constellation is Orion, the Hunter. Its stars are much brighter than those of the Plough, and make up a pattern which is easy to find. The two most brilliant stars in it have special Arabic names: Betelgeuse and Rigel. (These names may sound rather strange; Betelgeuse is often pronounced 'Beetle juice'!) Orion cannot always be seen. For some time around June, when it is summer in Britain, it is too near the Sun, so that it is above the horizon only during the daytime.

You will find that bright stars twinkle. This is not because they are really doing so; their light has to come to us through the Earth's air, and the air 'shakes' the light about. A star that is low down in the sky will twinkle more than one that is almost overhead because we are looking through a greater thickness of the Earth's atmosphere. Planets do not twinkle as much as stars, although when a planet is close to the horizon it may twinkle quite noticeably.

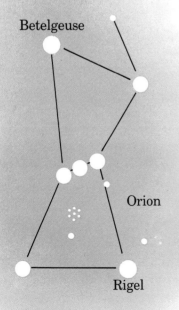

Constellation of Orion

Betelgeuse

Orion

Rigel

CHAPTER 13
THE CONSTELLATIONS

If you look up into a dark, clear sky, you may think that you can see millions of stars. This is not true. You can never see more than two or three thousand stars at any one time without using a telescope, and it is not hard to find your way around the sky, because the constellations always look the same.

Let us begin with the Great Bear or Plough, because it never sets over the British Isles. First find the Pole Star, which is also called Polaris, by using the two 'end' stars in the Plough. Next look for the Little Bear, which we might call the 'Little Plough' because it is rather the same shape, although it is much fainter. Apart from the Pole Star, it has only one fairly bright star.

If you look at the second star in the Plough 'handle', which is named Mizar, you will see that it has a much fainter star close beside it. Now begin at Mizar and imagine a line taken from it through the Pole Star. Follow on this line, and you will come to five fairly bright stars which make up a sort of W or M pattern. This is the constellation of Cassiopeia, which, like the Plough, never sets over Britain. (These names are not really difficult; you will soon get used to them.)

Now follow round the curve of the Plough handle, as shown here. Before long you will come to a very brilliant orange star, Arcturus in the constellation of the Herdsman. Unlike the Plough, it is not always visible, because it is further away from the pole of the sky, and spends some time below the horizon.

Orion, the Hunter, is on view during evenings all through winter and early

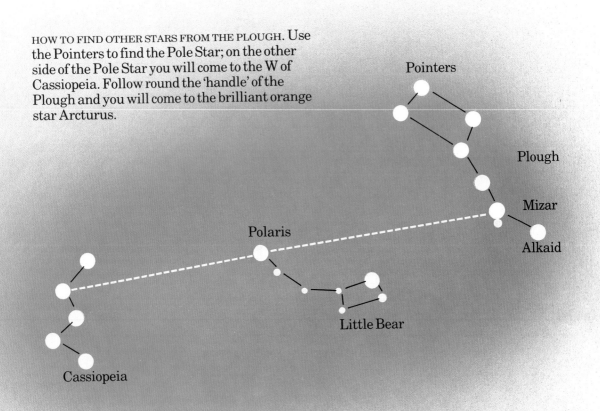

HOW TO FIND OTHER STARS FROM THE PLOUGH. Use the Pointers to find the Pole Star; on the other side of the Pole Star you will come to the W of Cassiopeia. Follow round the 'handle' of the Plough and you will come to the brilliant orange star Arcturus.

Pointers

Plough

Mizar

Alkaid

Polaris

Little Bear

Cassiopeia

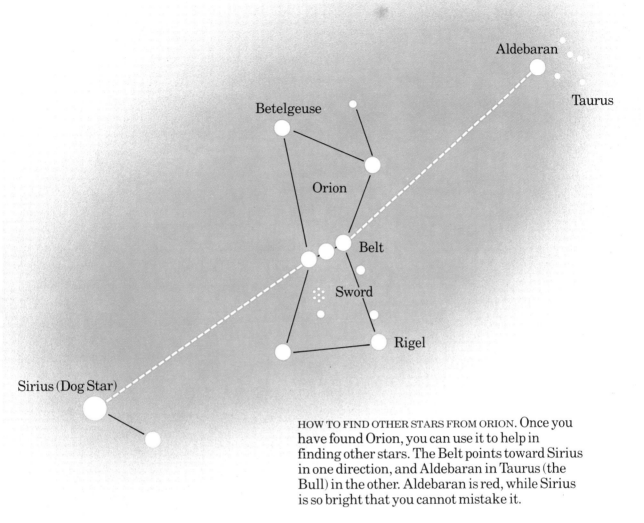

Aldebaran

Taurus

Betelgeuse

Orion

Belt

Sword

Rigel

Sirius (Dog Star)

HOW TO FIND OTHER STARS FROM ORION. Once you have found Orion, you can use it to help in finding other stars. The Belt points toward Sirius in one direction, and Aldebaran in Taurus (the Bull) in the other. Aldebaran is red, while Sirius is so bright that you cannot mistake it.

spring. I have already told you about its two brightest stars, Betelgeuse and Rigel; Betelgeuse is orange-red, while Rigel is pure white. The three stars in the middle of the constellation make up the Hunter's Belt, and if you follow the line from them upward you will reach another orange star, Aldebaran in the Bull. Downward, the stars in the Belt show the way to Sirius, which is much the brightest star in the whole of the sky (though it is not nearly so brilliant as some of the planets, such as Venus and Jupiter). Sirius is in the constellation of the Great Dog, and is often called the Dog Star.

Sirius is white, but when low down, as it always is when looked at from the British Isles, it seems to twinkle in different colours. It looks so bright because it is one of the closest of all the stars.

If you take a map of the stars and go outdoors when the sky is dark, you will soon learn how to find the different constellations. If you see a bright 'star' which is not on your Map, you may be sure that it is a planet. We cannot show the planets on our star maps, because they move about from one constellation to another.

CHAPTER 14
STORIES IN THE SKY

You may wonder how the constellations were named. The names of the most famous constellations were given thousands of years ago, and many of them come from the old stories that were being told then.

One of these stories is about the two Bears. The Great Bear was once a princess who was so beautiful that the queen of the gods, Juno, became jealous of her. One day, when the princess was walking in the woods near her home, Juno changed her into a bear. The princess's son had no idea that this had happened, and he had no way of finding out. Years later, when he was out hunting, he met the bear, and was just going to shoot it when the king of the gods, Jupiter,

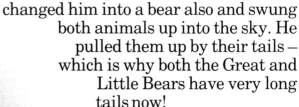

THE TWO BEARS. The group which we usually call the Plough is really part of a larger constellation, the Great Bear. The Little Bear has the Pole Star as its leader.

changed him into a bear also and swung both animals up into the sky. He pulled them up by their tails – which is why both the Great and Little Bears have very long tails now!

There is also a story about Orion, the great huntsman, who thought that he could kill any creature on earth. But he had forgotten the scorpion, which is quite small and very dangerous. One day a scorpion crawled out of a hole in the ground and stung Orion in the foot, so that he died – but Jupiter brought him back to life and put him in the sky. The Scorpion is there too, and is a very bright constellation, led by the

THE SCORPION. This is one of the few groups which really does look rather like the object after which it is named! The long line of bright stars, with the brilliant red Antares, can easily be said to look like a scorpion.

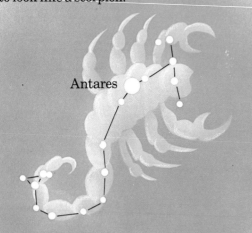

34

brilliant red star Antares. To make sure that the hunter and the scorpion could never meet again, they were put on opposite sides of the sky, so that they are always a long way apart.

In summer you can see a small constellation called the Dolphin. It was said that there once lived a great singer named Arion, whose voice was so beautiful that he won every competition in which he took part. Once when he was sailing home, bringing his prizes, the sailors thought that they would steal everything he had won. They threw Arion over the side of the ship, expecting that he would be drowned; but he was saved by a dolphin, which carried him safely to the beach. It is this dolphin that is now to be found in the sky.

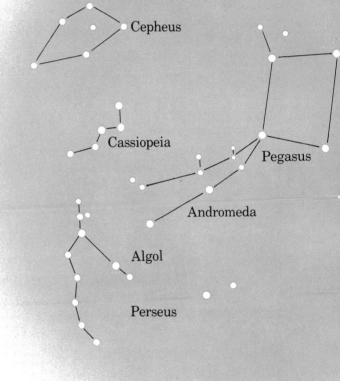

THE KING AND THE HERO. In the north of the sky we see all the characters of the Perseus legend: Perseus himself, with the Gorgon's head marked by the star Algol; the princess Andromeda; and the princess's parents, the king (Cepheus) and the queen (Cassiopeia).

The best-known of all the old stories is that of the princess and the sea monster. King Cepheus and his wife, Queen Cassiopeia, had a daughter called Andromeda, who was more beautiful than the daughters of the Sea God. The Sea God sent a monster to attack the country, and the king was told that the only way to save his people was to tie Andromeda to a rock on the edge of the sea and wait for her to be eaten by the monster. Luckily, she was saved by a hero called Perseus, who had been sent to kill a dreadful creature, Medusa, who had a woman's body and hair made of snakes. Medusa's head was so terrible that anybody looking at it would be turned into stone. Perseus showed the head to the sea monster, after which he married Andromeda and lived happily ever after. Perseus, Cepheus, Cassiopeia and Andromeda are all in the sky (we have already met Cassiopeia, marked by the W of stars not far from Polaris). Even the sea monster is there; nowadays we call it Cetus.

Of course these old stories are not true, but they are well worth reading, and it has been said that the sky is nothing more than a huge picture book.

35

CHAPTER 15
HOW FAR AWAY ARE THE STARS?

I have already told you that the stars are much further away than any of the planets. It is easy to work out a model to show what is meant. Let us say that the distance between the Sun and the Earth is given by the length of this line:

_____

On the same scale, the nearest star Proxima Centauri, would be more than 12 kilometres (7½ miles) away. It is no wonder that even very powerful stars look so much smaller and fainter than the Sun.

The first man to measure the distance of a star did so in the year 1838. His name was Friedrich Bessel, and he was a famous astronomer who lived in Germany.

Background stars

Measure of star distance (parallax) by movement against background stars due to Earth's movement around the Sun.

Nearby star

A   ○ Sun   B

Earth's orbit

To show how he did it, carry out a simple experiment. Close one eye, and then hold up a finger, lining it up with something a few yards away from you (such as a picture on the wall). Now, without moving your finger, close your first eye and open the other. Your finger will no longer be lined up with the picture, because you are looking at it from a different direction; your two eyes are not in the same place. If you know how much your finger seems to have moved, and you also know the distance between your eyes, you can work out how far your finger must be from your face.

Now think about the way in which the Earth moves round the Sun. We know that the distance between the Sun and the Earth is 150 million kilometres (93 million miles), so that from January to June, as the Earth moves from one side of its orbit to the other, it shifts by twice 150 million kilometres (93 million miles) – that is to say, 300 million kilometres (186 million miles).

Bessel chose a star in the constellation of the Swan which he thought might be closer than most of the other stars. He measured its position in January, and found that it was at the point marked A in the picture. Then he waited for six months, and measured the position again. This time the star was at B, while the other stars, which were much further away, seemed to be in the same positions as before.

Now he could draw up a triangle. He knew the distance which the Earth had moved (300 million kilometres – 186 million miles) and he also knew the amount by which the star had shifted, so that he could draw the whole triangle to scale and work out how far away the star must be. The idea is just the same as in the experiment you tried just now. Your eyes represent the positions of the Earth in January and June, and your finger represents the star which Bessel chose, while the picture on the wall stands for the more distant stars.

He found that the star's distance was so great that it could not easily be given in kilometres, just as it would be very clumsy to measure the distance between London and New York in millimetres. Astronomers usually give star distances in what are called 'light years'. Light moves along very quickly, at a rate of 300,000 kilometres (186 thousand miles) every second, so that in a year it can travel over 9 million million kilometres (more than 5½ million million miles). It is this distance that we term a light year (remember that a light year is a measure of distance, not of time). The star in the Swan turned out to be about 11 light years away.

The Scorpion

If light takes 11 years to reach us from this star, we must be seeing it as it used to be 11 years ago. Most of the other stars are much further away than this, and only a few are closer. The nearest of all bright stars beyond the Sun, Alpha Centauri, is just over 4 light years away.

Stars that are many light years from us do not appear to shift much because of the Earth's movement round the Sun, and we have to find other ways of measuring their distances. What astronomers do is to work out how bright they really are, and once this is known we can find out how far away they must lie. If you stand on the edge of the sea and see a light across the water, it may be a brilliant light a long way off or else a faint light near the shore; once you know how bright it *really* is, you can work out how far out to sea it is – and this is the same idea as that which astronomers use for the stars.

Rigel, the bright white star in Orion, is about 900 light years away, so that we are now seeing it as it used to be when William the Conqueror was King of England. On the other hand it takes light only eight and a half minutes to reach us from the Sun, and less than two seconds to reach us from the Moon.

CHAPTER 16
DIFFERENT KINDS OF STARS

The stars are of different colours, which means that they are not all equally hot. White stars such as Rigel or Sirius are hotter than our yellow Sun, while the Sun is hotter than red stars such as Betelgeuse or Aldebaran.

When a star is born, inside a gas-and-dust cloud, it is very cool, and at first it does not shine. As it becomes smaller it heats up, and when it is hot enough it starts to send out light. The Sun, as I have told you, shines because of changes taking place inside it, and most of the stars that you can see at night time are shining in just the same way.

But what happens when the 'fuel' of a star is used up? The inside of the star shrinks, and the outer parts swell out, cooling down.

1. Sun now

2. Red giant

3. Outer shell thrown off

4. White dwarf

THE LIFE OF A STAR. A star, such as the Sun, is born out of a cloud of dust and gas. It shrinks and becomes hot; it starts to shine, as the Sun is doing now (1). But it cannot last for ever. When it uses up its energy, the inside shrinks and the outside swells and becomes cool; the star turns into a red giant (2). Then it throws off its outer part, and we are left with a small, dense star surrounded by a huge shell of gas (3). When the gas has gone, the star becomes a very small white dwarf (4) which goes on shining very weakly until it becomes a cold, dead globe.

The star becomes a red giant, as Betelgeuse is now. The Sun will turn into a red giant one day, though not for thousands of millions of years yet. This is not the end. A star such as the Sun will throw off its outer parts, and what is left will become a very small, very heavy star called a white dwarf. White dwarfs are

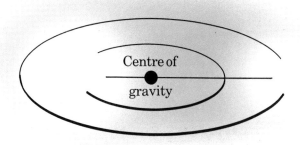

PAIRS OF STARS. Stars often are found in pairs, moving round each other, rather in the way of a dumbbell. The 'centre of movement' is always closer to the heavier star.

very strange things. If you could take a cup and fill it with material from a white dwarf, it would weigh several tons. After a still longer period the star will stop shining altogether, and will become a cold, dead ball.

If the star is much heavier than the Sun, it will not go through its life story in the same way. When it has used up all its 'fuel' it will explode, and throw off most of itself into space. This is what we call a *supernova*. They are not very common, and in our own star system we have not seen any since 1604, but in 1987 a supernova blazed out in a nearby star system – the Large Cloud of Magellan – and became easily visible without a telescope, though it was too far south in the sky to rise over Britain. One supernova, seen in 1054, became so bright that it could be found even in the daytime. We can still see what is left of it – a patch of gas which we call the Crab Nebula, because it has been said that the shape really is a little like that of a crab. In the middle of the gas patch there is a tiny object which is even smaller and heavier than a white dwarf. A cupful of it would weigh thousands of millions of tons.

Our Sun will never explode in this way, which is lucky for us. It shines quite steadily, and sends us just the right amount of light and heat. Some other stars are different; they brighten up and fade down again, so that we can see how they are behaving, and we call them variable stars. Some variable stars have periods of a few days or weeks, and the way in which they change tells us how brilliant they really are, after which we can find out their distances very easily.

We also come across double stars – real pairs, moving round each other much as the two bells of a dumbbell will do when twisted by the bar joining them. Mizar in the Plough has the faint star Alcor close beside it, which you can see on any clear night. If a telescope is used, Mizar itself is found to be made up of two stars, so close together that without a telescope they appear as one. Nowadays many thousands of these double stars are known, and sometimes they are very beautiful. Albireo, in the Swan (not the star measured by Bessel), is made up of a golden-yellow star and a companion which is bright blue.

Now and then a bright new star will blaze out in the sky. This is called a nova. It is quite different from a supernova; what happens is that a faint star suddenly flares up, staying bright for a few days, weeks or months before fading away again. All these exploding stars seem to be double, and it is the fainter member of the pair that flares up. The last bright nova was in the Swan. It appeared in 1976, and became more brilliant than the Pole Star, but it soon faded, and by now it has become so faint that you need a very powerful telescope to see it.

CHAPTER 17
STAR CLUSTERS AND STAR CLOUDS

Follow up the line of stars in Orion's Belt, and you will come to the bright orange Aldebaran, in the constellation of the Bull. Take the line still further, and you will reach what looks like a patch of mist in the sky. Look more carefully, and you will find that this patch is made up of stars. It is a true cluster; we often call it the Seven Sisters, because people with good eyesight can see at least seven stars in it, but astronomers call it the Pleiades. Binoculars show it very well, and with a telescope you can see a great many stars in it.

All the stars in the cluster are hot and white. We believe that they were born in the same way and in the same part of space, so that they have always stayed together; they are not nearly so old as the Sun, and will not last for so long before they use up their 'fuel'.

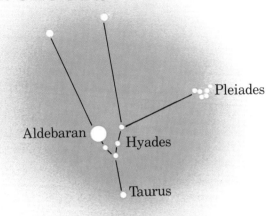

Pleiades

There are many other clusters of the same kind. Close to Aldebaran you will see some faint stars arranged in a V-shape. This is the Hyades cluster, which is less beautiful than the Seven Sisters although its stars are brighter. Aldebaran is not really a member of the cluster, but just happens to lie about halfway between the Hyades and ourselves. Another cluster is the Beehive, on the other side of Orion, and in the Southern Cross, never visible from the British Isles, we find the lovely Jewel Box, so named because it contains both blue and red stars.

Some clusters are of a different kind; there is one in the rather faint constellation of Hercules. This is what we call a *globular* cluster. The stars in it are arranged in a ball or globe shape, and there may be millions of

M13
Globular
Cluster

Hercules

Globular cluster in Hercules

them, so close together near the middle of the cluster that they cannot be seen separately – even though they are still too wide apart to be in danger of hitting each other. If we lived inside a globular cluster the night sky would be brilliant, with many stars bright enough to cast shadows, and there would be no darkness at all.

Next we come to the clouds of dust and gas which we call *nebulae* (the word *nebula* is Latin for 'cloud'). The best-known nebula is in Orion, below the three stars of the Belt. It is easy to see without a telescope as a misty glow, shining because of the stars mixed in with it. There are plenty of these nebulae, and we know that they are the places in which new stars are being born. The gas in them is millions of times less dense than the air we are breathing.

Orion Nebula

Look into the sky on a dark night, and you will see a bright band stretching from one horizon to the other. This is the Milky Way. Use a telescope, or a pair of binoculars, and you will find that the Milky Way is made up of stars – so many of them that it would be quite impossible to count them.

The star system in which we live is called the *Galaxy*. The Sun is only one of a hundred thousand million stars in it. The Galaxy is flattened in shape, rather like two fried eggs clapped together back to back, as shown in the picture, in which the Sun's position is at S. When we look from S towards A or B, we see many stars almost one behind the other, and this is what makes the Milky Way.

If we could look 'up' or 'down' on the Galaxy we would find that it is a spiral, like a Catherine wheel. The Sun, with the Earth and the other planets, lies near the edge of one of the spiral arms. The whole Galaxy is turning round; the Sun takes about 225 million years to make one full journey round the centre of the system. We cannot see the real centre of the Galaxy, because there is too much 'dust' in the way and the light from the centre is blotted out, just as a thick fog will make it impossible to see street lamps. We are not sure just what the centre of the Galaxy is like, but we know that it lies on the far side of the star clouds in the constellation of the Archer.

A negative photograph of a galaxy seen edge on and in plan which is a way that astronomers find it easier to look at stars.

CHAPTER 18
BEYOND THE MILKY WAY

All the stars you can see at night time belong to our Galaxy, which is so big that it would take a ray of light a hundred thousand years to cross from one side to the other.

Far away in space we can find other galaxies. They are of the same kind as ours, and some of them are even larger. One of the nearest is in the constellation of Andromeda (the beautiful princess of the story about the sea monster). The Andromeda Galaxy can just be seen without a telescope when the sky is really dark, and binoculars show it easily, but it looks like nothing more than a patch of light, and to see the stars in it we have to use photographs taken with powerful telescopes. Andromeda is over two million light years away, and it is spiral in shape, though it is tilted almost edge-on to us and we cannot make out the spiral form properly.

Galaxies are not always spiral; some of them are oval, while others have no definite shape at all. In them we find stars of all kinds, together with clusters, nebulae, and clouds of dark dust. Most of the galaxies are many millions of light years away, which is why they look so faint.

Andromeda Galaxy (M31)

Andromeda

Square of Pegasus

POSITION OF THE ANDROMEDA GALAXY. The Andromeda Galaxy is a very big system of stars; you can just see it with the naked eye and binoculars show it clearly.

The Andromeda Galaxy is made up of over 100 thousand million stars, and it is so far away that its light takes over two million years to reach us.

Except for a few of the very nearest systems, such as the Andromeda Galaxy, all the galaxies are moving away from us – and the further away they are, the faster they are going. The whole universe is spreading out or *expanding*.

The largest telescopes used today can show us galaxies which are so far away that their light takes thousands of millions of years to reach us; we are seeing them as they used to be before the Earth was born. But how far can we go? Is there an end to the universe?

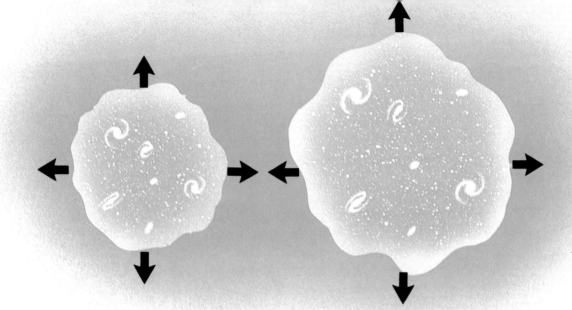

HOW THE UNIVERSE IS SPREADING OUT. All the groups of galaxies are moving quickly away from each other, so that the universe is expanding or spreading-out .

The Sun is an ordinary star, and it seems likely that other stars too have planets moving round them. Unfortunately we cannot see planets of other stars, because they are too faint, but we have some evidence that they exist. Some stars appear to be 'pulled' by planets, so that they shift very slightly in the sky – though these shifts are much too small to be noticed except when measured with very powerful instruments.

This is a question that we cannot yet answer. It is hard to see how space can come to an end. If it does, then what is outside it? But if it does not end, we have to try to picture something that goes on for ever and ever, which again we cannot do. Neither can we decide just how the universe began. Most astronomers believe that everything appeared suddenly about fifteen thousand million years ago, and that the universe started to spread out at once. The galaxies were formed, then the stars, and then planets such as the Earth. Unfortunately, there seems to be no way in which we can find out just how the universe itself was born.

Another question that we cannot yet answer is a very important one: Is there any life in the universe except on the Earth? We have not found any, and we are now sure that there is no other life in the Solar System – probably not even on Mars, which in some ways is not too unlike the Earth. But we must always remember that the stars are suns, and it is hard to believe that our Sun is the only one to have a family of planets. If there are other Earths moving round other stars, there seems no reason to doubt that life may exist on them.

We cannot send rockets to the stars, because it would take much too long. At the moment we have no idea of how we can travel far into space, but it is true to say that the men of a few hundred years ago would have been just as unable to send pictures through the air, as we do today with our television.

One day, perhaps, we may get in touch with 'other men' on the planets of other stars. We must wait and see.

CHAPTER 19
BECOME AN ASTRONOMER!

In this book I have tried to tell you something about astronomy, and about the universe in which we live. It is a wonderful place, and there is always something new to see. So why not take up astronomy as a hobby, as I did when I was six years old?

I can give you some advice. First, read some more books, and find out as much as you can. Then go outdoors at night (taking care not to lose your way in the darkness), and start learning the constellations, which should not take you very long. If you can borrow a pair of binoculars, look at the Moon with its mountains and its dry seas; look at the coloured stars, the double stars, and the clusters and star clouds as well as the Milky Way. If you are still keen, then join an astronomy club. Most towns have clubs of their own, and you will make many new friends.

You may be lucky enough to have a telescope. If so, then you will be able to start proper observing. Even if this is not possible, you can still make a hobby out of astronomy, and I know that you will enjoy it.

I wish you the best of luck!

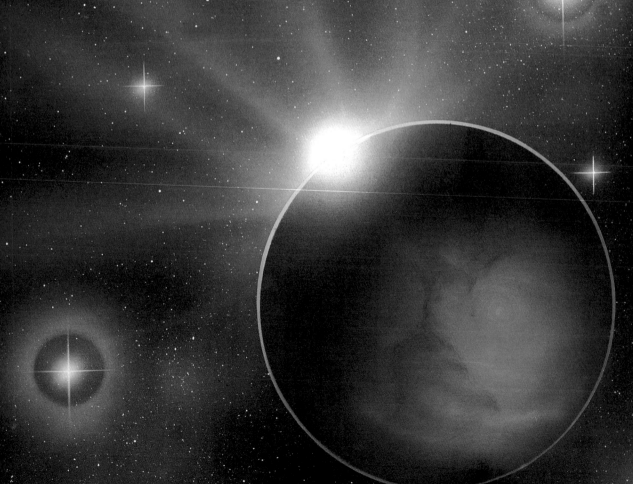

ABOVE A Planisphere will show you the position of the stars at any time of day. Planispheres are available to cover many latitudes.

Recommended binoculars for young astronomers – a 7 × 50 and a 10 × 50.

CHAPTER 20
TEST YOUR SKILL

I wonder how much you have learned about astronomy by now? Most people enjoy testing themselves, so here are a few questions for you. You will find all the answers earlier in this book.

1. Which is bigger – the Sun or the Moon?
2. What is the name of the comet that comes back every 76 years?
3. Which moon of Jupiter is red, with volcanoes on it?
4. What is the name astonomers give to the Seven Sisters?
5. Name the brightest star in the sky.
6. What colour is the planet Saturn?
7. In which constellation are Betelgeuse and Rigel?
8. Can you ever see the Southern Cross from Britain?
9. From Britain, when will we see the next total eclipse of the Sun?

10. Is the surface of the planet Venus hotter or colder than that of the Earth?

11. Which planet looks like a red star when you look at it without a telescope?

12. What is an asteroid?

13. What is the proper name of the constellation which we often call the Plough?

14. Which is the closest planet to the Sun?

15. What shape is the Andromeda Galaxy?

16. Name the German astronomer who first measured the distance of a star.

17. Which is the planet with the bright rings?

18. In the old story, who was the great singer who was rescued by a dolphin?

19. Does the Moon have any light of its own?

20. What is the best time of the year to look for meteors?

If you have a score of more than 15 out of 20, you are doing well. I have given the answers at the very end of this book – but do not cheat and look them up before you have tried to answer the questions!

Useful information

The Planets

Planet (Mean Distance from the Sun, in millions of –)			Sidereal Period ('year')	Axial Rotation ('day')	Diameter (equatorial)		No. of moons
	km	miles			km	miles	
Mercury	58	36	88 days	58.7 days	4,880	3,033	0
Venus	108	67	225 days	243 days	12,107	7,523	0
Earth	150	93	365.26 days	23h 56m	12,756	7,925	1
Mars	228	141.5	687 days	24h 37m	6,787	4,218	2
Jupiter	778	483	11.9 years	9h 50m	142,984	88,865	16
Saturn	1427	886	29.5 years	10h 39m	120,536	74,914	20
Uranus	2870	1783	84 years	17h 14m	51,118	31,770	15
Neptune	4497	2793	164.8 years	17h 52m	50,538	31,410	2
Pluto	5900	3667	247.7 years	6 days 9h	2,324	1,444	1

The Brightest Stars

Star	Constellation	Magnitude*	Luminosity Sun = 1	Distance Light years	Colour
Sirius	Great Dog	−1.5	26	8.8	White
Canopus	Keel	−0.7	200,000	1200	White
Alpha Centauri	Centaur	−0.3	1.5	4.3	White
Arcturus	Herdsman	−0.1	115	36	Orange
Vega	Harp	0.0	52	26	Blue
Capella	Charioteer	0.1	70	42	Yellow
Rigel	Orion	0.1	60,000	900	White
Procyon	Little Dog	0.4	11	11	White
Achernar	River	0.5	780	85	White
Betelgeuse	Orion	var.	15,000	310	Orange-red
Agena	Centaur	0.6	10,500	460	White
Altair	Eagle	0.8	10	17	White
Acrux	Southern Cross	0.8	3,200	360	White
Aldebaran	Bull	0.8	100	68	Orange
Antares	Scorpion	1.0	7,500	330	Red
Spica	Virgin	1.0	2,100	260	White

(Canopus, Alpha Centauri, Achernar, Agena and Acrux are too far south in the sky to be seen from Europe or the northern United States)

*Magnitude is a measure of a star's apparent brightness. The lower the magnitude the brighter the star. Four stars have magnitudes below 0, so that they have **minus** values; these are the four most brilliant stars in the sky.

Answers to quiz on previous pages

1. The Sun is much bigger than the Moon.
2. Halley's Comet.
3. Io.
4. The Pleiades.
5. Sirius.
6. Yellow.
7. Orion.
8. No; it is too far south in the sky.
9. On 11 August 1999.
10. Much hotter.
11. Mars.
12. A very small planet. Most asteroids move between the orbits of Mars and Jupiter.
13. The Great Bear (Americans call it the Big Dipper).
14. Mercury.
15. Spiral.
16. Friedrich Bessel.
17. Saturn.
18. Arion.
19. No; it depends only upon being lit up by the Sun.
20. August.

Illustration acknowledgments

Paul Doherty illustrations: 23, 29, 40 (top), 44
Paul Doherty photograph: 17 (bottom), 21 (top), 41
John Fairweather: 16
Patrick Moore Collection: 13 (2), 17 (top), 18, 30, 40 (bottom), 42

NASA: 19 (2), 21 (bottom), 25 (2)
George Philip Ltd: 45
Royal Astronomical Society: 28
J.J. Vickers & Son Ltd: 45